Phoenixes Groomed as Genesis Doves

Jasmine Farrell

Copyright©2016-2022 Jasmine Farrell

Fourth Edition, Paperback-
Published December 2022
Previously published through Pomegranate Press
January 2016

All rights reserved.
Printed in the United States of America
No part of this book may be reproduced in any
written, electronic, recording, or photocopying form
without written permission of the author,
Jasmine Farrell.

ISBN- 978-1-7379460-2-1

Dedication

To: *Fellow Phoenixes*

Acknowledgements

I would like to thank my family and friends who have supported me through the years. I'm thankful for my spouse, Reign for encouraging me to keep going until my hands cease moving and my heart stops beating. I am thankful for my father. Daddy, you are a rock that I thank the divine for every day. To my Auntie Momo…I love you so much and I'm so glad I have a gem like you in my life. You are a blessing for real. Keneil and Olivia, thank you for sticking beside me during this journey. Kim, Tedra, Jhajha, Rosebud, Amarii, Zhane'l, Gaby, and Dor …Thank you for your support, ears, eyes and, patience.

Preface

When creating this book(2014-2016), I began going through a process of liberating myself from toxic habits, childhood faiths, self-doubt and bitterness. I was and still am transitioning from various schools of thought and the lack thereof.

I wanted to organize my poems in the order of these transitions. I categorized the other poems based on their topics. I wanted to leave everything in black and white. Pen not included. From heartbreak to leaving imaginary boxes, I wanted to leave it on the page. I had many doubts releasing this book because of cognitive dissonance haunting the way I hungered to step into new ideals and transform for the better. I was terrified of the judgment I would receive from family members, mentors and old acquaintances; however, that is also the reason I released this book. There are many out there who are dealing with the same issues and feelings I expressed in these poems.

It took me two years to write these poems. As diary entries, I scribbled my feelings, observations and truth, without sugar, into my little poetry journal. When I realized that these poems were telling my story, I began typing them up and organizing them. I sent the original manuscript of only thirty poems, to a few friends. I pushed my miniature manuscript to the back of my mind until I was given the opportunity to publish it. I then continued to expand and write more poems.

I bled my heart out in black ink, hoping someone could relate, laugh, cry and feel motivated.

The best way I can express my experiences and share the little goodies of wisdom I've learned, (sometimes the hard way) from what I've experienced, is through poetry.

Table of Contents

I've Always Wanted to be a Poet 1

Letter to the Pretentious Poets 3

The Shift 5

I am Livin' (For Zora) 6

The R Train Phoenix 8

Lover of Autumn 10

Don't Give Up 12

For the Sunsets We Don't Talk About 13

Determination 15

There Will Be Days 16

Lil' Ol' Letter to My Readers 18

Cranberry, Church, and Vodka 19

To the Phoenixes Groomed as Genesis Doves 20

One Light. Many Candles 22

Blossoming Black Hybrid 23

Resist 26

Lil' Ol' Prayer 27

God Is 28

The Essentials	29
The Forever Muse	31
Musk	33
Serene's Coffee Shop	34
Nikki	37
Infatuation	38
Behaved Phoenix	39
She Is Beautiful.	40
Heavy to Carry	42
Cherry-Colored Casket	44
Ruby	46
Dear 1960s	48
Have a Sense of Humor!	50
The Majority Rant	52
Arrogant in their Ignorance	54
Whispering Alarm Clock	55
Unhidden and Unaddressed	56
Listen, Lady Phoenix	58
Mister	61
Chaos	62
BackBiters	63
The Quiet Ones	64

Turn of Events	66
For the Carefree Mornings	67
Diane	69
Ms. Lady	70
Raine	71
Bashir	72
Let Go	73
The Morning After	74
Grass Ain't Finna Be Greener	76
Dominique	78
Annie Ruth	79
Ma!	82
Secrets	85
To the Wonder Women Clan	87
How I'm Doin'	90

I've Always Wanted to be a Poet

I've always wanted to be a poet.
A master of metaphors,
stretching out experiences
one line at a time.
Bleed in black ink,
letting strangers
know
they are not alone.

Peel off identities
society has thrown at them.
Show them how brightly they shined
way before the ache came in,
way before they realized that
not all monsters are big and scary.
Sometimes,
the beasts are loved ones
in proper attire
with bright-eyed smiles and
snake-like tongues.

I've always wanted to be a poet.
A deity of exhortation and dope parallels.
The one who uses *like* or *as*
with comparisons, but refuses to call it a simile
because I'm just so
mushy and deep
—
Yeah, that kind of poet.

Make the pen ink proud of me,
the paper pissed at my emotions
for sojourning within the four corners
so aggressively and poignant.

Place literary concoctions
into the hands of those
who know what it's
like to have lovers
tear their heart to pieces and then ask,
"Who hurt you?"
Give them the courage to face
their monsters poetically
while writing how I faced my own.

Oh, I've always wanted to be a poet.
A master of metaphors.
Keeper of priceless personifications,
creating neon syllables with my tongue.
Enticing ears to listen to my lil'
ol' perception of life, its details,
its luster and lack thereof.
Stretching out my experiences one line at a time.

Letter to the Pretentious Poets

I am not sure if you're aware…
Your arrogance is leaking
from your pretentious thighs.
When you switch your hips,
I hear your ego and insecurities rub together
like foxy big boys who are overtly vain.
You belittle anyone who crosses your path.
Sacrificing the dignity
and the creativity of others,
you coddle your degrees with
condescending statements so foggy
and watered down,
condensation is jealous.
        You breathe in wicked affirmations
                and
          exhale malevolence as they
          kiss your golden-painted ass.
          Placed on a pedestal so high,
          they can't see the paint chipping.
          They think you're raining down
          golden leaves of gratitude.

I am not sure if you know this:
Poetry is not an exclusive expression
for the elite imposters and puffed-up degrees.

It's for anyone who has overcame.
Anyone who speaks of victory from the debris.
It's for the least, it's for the greatest.

We honor the late poets
and give the new one's patience.
Poetry is for the lost,
poetry is for the found.
You can't frown upon a poetic device
'cause your lofty eyes
and ears can't comprehend its distinctive flow.
Poetry fits in boxes, triangles and octagons.
It bursts out of boxes, triangles and octagons.
It beats out truth and whispers lies.
Rips hearts and guards souls.
I don't care what you were told,
poetry is too big of an art to confine.
I know you think your receding hair line
gives you a right to speak your narrow-minded
creativity, but I literally can't hear your perception
        through your intimidation of the
                unknown
           flows, visuals and prose.
I suppose you should go meditate and grow with a
diverse crowd.
That way,
your humility may be found...

The Shift

Peeling off wounded fears
like dead skin from sun burns.

When I was a little girl,
I wished
under the polluted palette of midnight.
Wished to travel so deep within,
I'd reach dreams
secretly hidden within my soul.
Wished that dreams from star dust, stories
and soul-glow would be reality.

Oh, how I wished.
I was afraid until my core peeled
away the past hurts
like dead skin from sun burns.
My...
how things are beginning to change.

I am Livin' (For Zora)

"Jasmine, what are you doin'?"
I'm embracing the winter chill.
Struttin' up a Harlem Street
under a navy-blue sky.
I'm swaying to a honey voice
and string instruments.
Lovely, my sacral felt
like it was gonna ooze
out of my pores.
Honey, I'm livin'.

I'm romancing my essence
to the guitar riffs from the captain.
Freedom found in the basement of Nabe.
Live concoctions of healing,
internal rhyming joy, after every note.
I am forgivin' old lovers,
past hurts and self-sabotage
with the boisterous drum kit.
Pulsating my torso and lifting my hands
to the samba drum.
I am livin'.

Me, myself and I,
floating on the rhythmic vibes,
I'm sure past generations
know everything about.
Freedom found in two-steppin'.

Capturing peace with wild spins and heavy slides.
I dip to the down beats 'cause joy is hidden there.
No need to grin, I'm sprinklin' spirit fingers.
Honey,
you
know
how
I
feel.
Dippin' low,
letting go of *shoulda, coulda, wouldas.*
Bringin' up courage of the unknown
and leavin' my comfort zone.
Honey, I am livin'.

The R Train Phoenix

There was this obnoxious confidence
that coated her sweetly selfless heart.
Head lowered in a book,
my eyes snuck glances at her
fierce hands,
I'm sure they felt like thirty years of nurturing
and forty-five years of self-loving.

I didn't need to know her
to know that she'd been introduced
to the secrets of quiet summer nights
and the flinging off of grudges
like tightly-strapped bras.
She knew magic.

Faery kisses on her nails,
wands tied at the ends of her braids.
Eyes brightly honey hazel, hoisting unspoken syllables
that can serenade grizzly bears
out of hibernation
just to hear her speak.
I listened.

Deeply engaged in freeing her friend
without having to cast any spells
—
She speaks.

She speaks fables we're all afraid to face.
Lips shining glitter and fantasies,
she uttered softly, but sharp enough to hear,
"My father was the first one to break my heart.
He was the first person I forgave."

I didn't need to know her to know
she'd been introduced
to the secrets of quiet summer nights
and the flinging off of grudges
like tightly strapped bras.
She knew peace.

Spider legs at the corners of her eyes,
shiny laugh lines,
quiet wrinkles on her forehead...
She knew the passwords for every troll bridge.
She knew magic.

I didn't need to know her
to know she burned brightly hundreds
of times
and laughed within her own ashes.
Her giggles were victorious.
Arms flapping rapidly after every sentence
she proclaimed of forgiveness,
heartache and the mystics of time.
She knew magic.

Lover of Autumn

I was once the girl
yearning to dance
when the sun began to peak its head
but
weighed herself down by what she was taught
and
refused to be uplifted by what was in her heart.
No more.

I shimmy at sunrise.
Wiggle like flowers
whenever rain storms water petals.
Bounce my footsteps to the hissing
of the trees with the auburn leaves.
It's the little things, I guess.

Snap my fingers to the cracking
of acorns from heavy and sexy heels.
Slow dance when viewing
the color palette of dusk
and hum with the rising of the moon.
I don't withhold self-love from myself.

I was once the girl
yearning to be herself.
Envied the creatures who radiated
sidewalks, clicking their shoes,
squeaking their sneakers

on pavements without apologies.
I walked lightly.
Ashamed of my own footsteps.
Watched phoenixes soar through the winter breeze,
burn brightly during the autumn season
and rest on cherry blossom trees.
                       No more.

I adore my scarred wings in the morning
and polish my beak by noon.
Let the moonlight settle my soul,
hushing nighttime thoughts.
Force the morning hush to reawaken
what cognitive dissonance
puts to sleep at night.
Get my shoulders ready for the sun.
Cause,
hot damn,
I love to shimmy with life.

Don't Give Up

Dying to give into defeat.
Occasionally, a wind whispers "You, you're nothing."
Numbing the pain with temporary fill-ins sounds nice.
Tempted to cope with substances making circumstances worse.
Going against the grain was never an easy plight.
Instead of going the easy route, you chose freedom.
Victory always has a story that has a few hurricanes.
Eventually, the sun will come out- you'll find ease.
Unify your hunger with your current pain.
Press on with your goal tattooed underneath your eyelids.

For the Sunsets We Don't Talk About

I've watched stars glisten in your eyes.
I've seen the sun set on your dreams.
It seems life has a way
of keeping us on our toes.
You chose to give into defeat,
now you shamefully shuffle through life.

Life has a way of peeling off joy
and stealing our hopes.
You've coped with long work hours
and repeated shrugs of compromise.
The bags under your eyes
make the bag ladies
on early Saturday mornings
look dainty and weak-handed.

I hope you understand
that life has its seasons
and spring maybe
taking its time to see you—
Just know the flowers will bloom
beautifully once it reaches you.

I've watched stars glisten
in your eyes and I've seen
the sun set on your dreams,

but please receive this poem
to keep going until a warm sunrise
arrives on your dreams.

Your journey isn't worthless
and your dark seasons are worth this
beautiful path you're walking on
to the satisfying destination
you're meant to reach.

Determination

Destined for something.
Everybody is called to shine in their own way.
There isn't one purpose greater than the other.
Every assignment is imperative.
Run towards your purpose without seeking incentives.
Marinate in the journey and never look back
Invite loved ones for the ride.
Never be ashamed of your past or hide.
Always keep going.
Take a few breaks if you have to.
Intertwine your passion with a little desperation.
Overtly shower those who were in your corner with love.
Never give up.

There Will Be Days

There will be days when the sun
will intimidate my comfort zone-
I'll let it.
I'll surrender to thoughtful justifications
and conniving escape plans to run
from whom I'm meant to be.

There will be days when past skeletons
will attempt to annihilate my spirit,
cease my chase to catch
my dreams while I'm awake.

There will be days when corpses
will attempt to identify with the
Transformation-pending-me.
Remind me of my "limits" and fears
and the years of wasted time on catering
to my neglect of self.

There will be days when my mind
will hate the change I'm walking into.
The war between old, new, and true
reigns heavily within my thoughts
on these days.

There will be days when painful wounds
will hold me close
and remind me that it has loved

me since I was four years old.
That it will always love me as long
as I don't allow RISK to separate us,
as long as I don't allow
PEACE to break us up.

There will be days when tears will not suffice.

I will always conquer those days.
Even if I win the battle battered and lost,
bitter and tossed to the side by everyone.
I will conquer those days
and make new ones that kiss HOPE
like a make-out session in France...

Lil' Ol' Letter to My Readers

I decided to listen
to what my heart was saying
and found peace.
Gave into following my dreams
and now I am more at ease.
Decided to live unapologetically.
My quintessence will not go
through bereavement while I'm still livin'.
I apologized to my true essence,
now all is forgivin'.
Spoke too many self-denying words
over myself that battered my insides.
Gave careless folk faux smiles
while despair cried behind my eyelids.
I am now conceiving the idea
my Auntie Momo once told me.
"Just live for you happily, without wondering what they think."
I hope you take heed and let this poem sink in.
Be yourself and stop self-denying
your awesomeness to fit in.
Love yourself from within
and adore your external beauty.
The people who throw stones
at you are the bitter ones…usually.
Live, love, forgive, give and laugh.
Don't forget to eat well
and surpass what they say about you.
You're cooler than the Yeti building Igloos.
And, if nobody loves you, know that I do.

Cranberry, Church, and Vodka

It's midnight.
I'm drunk.
My thighs are cold.
I'm attempting to
say my affirmations backwards
because, apparently,
at the moment, it sounds more dope.
I just left Church Bar
walking up the streets of
Church Avenue
to the Church Avenue train station
to take the F train home.
It's more allegorical than it is ironic.
If you only knew my journey…
I am evolving from what was
and it is the loneliest walk
of my life.
But it's best to walk solo
than with packs
who feed off your radiance,
rather than cuddling their own.
Vodka and Cranberry can never
soothe that kind of truth out of my mind.

To the Phoenixes Groomed as Genesis Doves

I know what it's like.
Your wings trimmed down
since you were an eggling.
Squawked words
of unprecedented paths they frowned upon.
You had to be caged.
Secular ruminations of spreading
your God-given wings-
it was mandated to be tamed.

I know what it's like...
To scream your truth into pillows
and meditate on beastly
lies
until you believe them to be
more authentic than your very soul.

Oh, honey, I know.
To be swayed to proudly walk in shame
of how bright you were destined to glow.
To be told to shine
but, only as much as you were told.

To the Phoenixes groomed to be Genesis doves,
I know what it's like.
To eventually clip your wings
and strip off your coat of vibrant colors.
To ignore the chills that tickled your sides.

You knew it was your soul.
It was beginning to itch.

I know what it's like.
But after a while, Phoenix…
Your feathers will be too tough to cut,
too vivacious to blend,
and your voice too boisterous to muzzle.

To the Phoenixes who were groomed to be Genesis doves,
I know what it's like.
To be belittled by those who reside
in your heart for being yourself
without apologies.
To be burned so maliciously
for not fitting into their cages,
you thought you were Lucifer's spouse.
To be so afraid of the aftermath,
you were ashamed of your own ashes.
Your cinders rattled, shook,
squirmed on the solid concrete.
Resurrecting from your own ashes,
you puffed out your Phoenix chest.

This time around,
soar high to the sun,
love the way you were supposed to.
Color the world bodacious
and peculiar like you were meant to.
Keep your feathers clean
and neon pretty
like rainbow fish in clear blue waters.

One Light. Many Candles

One day, a woman of the Islamic faith,
veiled divinely and poised,
prayed two feet away from me.
There was a pulling
from my spirit to hers.
A connection.
An epiphany snuck up on me
like little third graders tucked
under pastel wall corners
and they scream out "boo!"
A connection:
We're all communicating to the same divine entity
just a different name.
But us humans added manipulation,
separation, and games.
One light, many candles; it's all the same.
I've got a holistic view.
Old circles will believe
I'm screwed up in the head.
But I'm at ease at night when I go to bed.
My spirituality is a bit different, but I'm at peace.
At least I am no longer afraid to declare my lenses.
I've got a holistic view.
Same spirit, just a different view.
Same truth that heals with perfection if you let it.
I confess, I am no longer boxed in
and I don't regret it.

Blossoming Black Hybrid

She doesn't have skeletons in her closet.
She drapes them over her shoulders elegantly.
Smiles gently.

What lies beneath hums musingly.
Red roots anchor her unwritten doctrines.
Taunted by the righteous to never speak her gospel.
Her slivered truth.
Don't speak.
Smile gently.

Didn't blend in the background,
she crept underneath it.
Hoping her radiance would dim
like Marcy project light bulbs praying to be replaced…
She is captivating and it scares her.

Her hypnotizing aura of calm winds
was poison to a familial beast.
Hungry for fragile porcelain on sail boats.
Fiddled tea cups as he floated on his back.
Ran his fingers down her
little curves of fine China and laughed.
Didn't care that he was causing chaotic
sea storms and she was ages 6 to 11…
Or at least that's what she remembers.
And… another disturbance at 15.

Repeated offender.
Consistent with his tainted hands
on her third grader skin.
Yet her sin of secular music, free movements,
self-assurance sashaying down hallways
was just too heavy to ignore.
> ***Don't let the Enemy use you.***

Razor blade hickeys on her wrist
from midnight make-out sessions.
Her voice whispered through
the bleeding slits but never seemed to escape her lips.
Non-escaping thoughts of eternally sleeping.
> ***Smile gently.***

Mandatory self-denial to be a part of this club.
Your remission of self;
I mean sins.
Isolation from the world;
I mean sins.
Belittling, discrimination, patriarchal pride and misogyny;
> ***I mean standing up for the good book will get you through.***
> ***Appease the leaders.***
> ***Don't question, smile gently.***

If we're receptive, life will reveal
the monsters that kiss our lips
that sang us lullabies that held us close
with the claws hidden inside

their fists… just in case we resist.
Don't let the Enemy use you.

She saw the daunting lies
proudly reeking from their flesh.
Blindly nodding to generational rituals
and ascetic elitism.
Stripped off the indignity they dressed her in,
ripped out the stitches of self-denial
and unaddressed pain,
crawled out of their carnally pious grave.
Introverted—
glowing in corners, bleeding on pages,
glowing in the cracks, sashaying down hallways,
rolling down hills of peace.
Smile brightly.

She doesn't have skeletons in her closet.
She drapes them over her shoulders elegantly.
Smiles brightly.

Brushes her hands over her frame of dark stories
and laughs.
Feeds the broken her journey
and embraces her past.
Gives her voice to those willing to listen.
Leaves no remission of her human illuminating.
She is captivating and it doesn't scare her anymore.

Resist

Chicken skin with heart flames like the underworld.
Live freely and you will burn.
Follow those heartfelt footsteps
and you'll be kissing peace
in the abyss.
Resist.

Resist the temptation to live without the target being perfection.
Bless them with your freedom,
don't second guess their judgment.
Their self-proclaimed heaven-sent thoughts.
They'll tell you about your chicken skin but skimp on
your blazing soul that lights up dead hearts
with your pure intentions.
"How dare you walk your unknown path with your birthright love in your heart? Be careful," they'll say.
They'll try to snatch you off
your glitter glistening
road and coerce you to join their own.
Wicked leading the innocently blind.
Follow those heartfelt footsteps
and you'll be kissing peace in a man-made abyss.
Resist.

Resist the temptation to live without the target of perfection.
Bless them with your freedom.
Don't second guess.
Ignore the trumpet blaring
from the center of your chest.
Shoo away the intuitive caution signs and follow.

Lil' Ol' Prayer

God, gimme peace.
Like still summer mornings in Savannah peace.
Chase my worries to one corner of my mind.
Steady my anxious heart
and parallel its beats to morning drums...
Gimme serenity.

God Is...

God is…
not some exclusive being in the V.I.P section.
He is not the meek maintenance
employee in the bathroom lounge.
God is the music.
Some of us shimmy to it.
Some of us awkwardly surrender
our entire bodies to the bass.
Others slow whine
and some meditate on the beat
while boppin' their heads.
Some don't move at all and don't care.
No matter what you do, it still plays.
Still seeps through speakers.

The Essentials

Joy is
smiling at the sun
wondering if your eyes could taste its
shine,
the random cackle in the kitchen
from an embarrassing moment
you thought you'd never survive from.

Understanding is
keeping the light on for the lost, while the found
reminisce the days they wandered like nomads
harboring pretty jewels.
It's looking within your own pain for a few spells just to meet
the wounded where they are.

Peace is
allowing your heart to hum with the silence
and burst your brilliance in the noise.
It's the ancient oak tree roots unmoved by impossible hurricanes
and unforeseen tornadoes.

Love is
seizing the dirt from diamonds that were always tossed
aside like the simplistic coals they appeared to be.
It's perfectly smiling at the rain clouds and the

rainbows,
equally cheesy and bright.

Faith is
telling your monsters,
"You are nothing more than low lives lurking in hallways at 11pm."
It's the funny shaking and rumbling in your gut
reminding you
that you'll get through this
like Moses and the Red Sea.

Support is
looking past the potential, the present, and cupping
the soul as though it were the good berries
from Grandma Simpson's Garden.
It's falling without the fear of being alone
if you hit the ground—
when you hit the ground.

Beauty is
your smile when you finally know your worth.
It's the chaotic loss in exchange for something greater.
It's the perfection of acceptance--the fullness of everything.

The Forever Muse

It's been a little over a year
and
I still cry tears as if
the story of Noah's ark depended on it.
Thank God for the changing pattern
of the tides.
The highs and lows, the crazy waves of regrets
sinking me to the ocean floor.
High tides that catapult me to the clouds and
deliver me from deep ruminations of you.
I still reminisce the first time
I saw you enter a room:
Hands jammed in your pockets
like you had nothing to prove.
Your brandy-painted skin intoxicated my
quintessence
as your eyes
uttered sweet nothings before you even parted your
lips.
Hot damn…
how I loved your eyes.
I didn't have butterflies.
But who needs butterflies
when you can open blocked heart chakras
by merely uttering bass-dripping syllables?
Sadly, you left it in critical condition,
with your name graffitied around the borders.
But,

you didn't break my heart.
You bruised it senselessly
and expected me to be receptive to your
dollar store justifications.
It's been a little over a year
and I'm still trying to be okay with knowing
that when the stillness was so eerie
and the loneliness overcame you like a
spiritual possession,
I wanted to be the little voice to let you know
that you were not alone.
I'm still trying to be okay with the truth
that all you wanted to know
was what my honey dew melon morning dew
felt like slamming against
the vintage mahogany headboard.
It's been a little over a year
and I'm still glad that you
NEVER got a chance to know.
It's been a little over a year
and I'm still rambling poetically.
Bleeding in black ink refusing to band-aid
the wound with Al Green songs
and ice cream.
It's been a little over a year
and you're still one of my greatest muses,
most hated inspirations
and the source of hundreds of poems.
I'm okay with that.
I like poems.

Musk

You're my favorite.
From your eyes to your smile,
down to your essence.

Serene's Coffee Shop

I learned the art of masking just for you.
So, whenever you saw my face,
you'd struggle to see the ache burning
beneath my eyelids
or
the desperation to feel your lips again.
I forgot to glue my ceramic cheeks back together
after seeing you months later,
standing in line at
Serene's Coffee Shop.

You wore dark blue jeans that fit you loosely,
adjacent to the love you had for me.
You didn't utter a word.
But your face wanted to say everything.
Nose flared and flesh red like stolen rubies.
Your lashes wouldn't stop beating each other
as your eyes were trying to find
words to say.
You gulped down guilt
like iced coffee on Mondays.
Your hands-
Your hands...
tapping the sides of your thighs.
You began to tap your foot and I realized
the allegory of your foot
and the tears beneath this mask of mine.

Maybe you didn't know
that my heart was not
a piece of the concrete
the day you told
me your sugarless truth.
Maybe you were too preoccupied
with soothing your ego
with my defensively fragile heart.
I yearned to run into your arms
in Serene's Coffee Shop.
Instead, I grinned from the distance
with my glass joy and painted peace,
placed poised and pretty on my face.
I blinked two times and waved.
Thought about the day
you told me your sugarless truth.
You waved back and saw
the cracks on my ceramic cheeks.
You peeped the pain aggressively
attempting to crawl
out from the cracks.
I turned away and waved once more.
I learned the art of masking just for you.
So, whenever you saw my face,
you'd struggle to see the ache
burning beneath my eyelids
or
the desperation to feel your lips again.
My high ceramic cheek bones
and glossed grin covers the truth that:

I will always love the way you
do every damn thing
like heroes on their journey
to a victory that's damn near impossible
to reach.

Nikki

When the sun kissed your dimple
through the windows, past the curtains
and your bed sheets,
I almost lost my mind in awe.
I wonder if those gorgeous dents came after she left
or after she cheated for the third time.
The third time's the charm.
No.
The third time, the alarm
at the base of your intuition is broken
and your common sense has left you.
Your best you now hide underneath walls so thick,
I'm sure steel is jealous.
I wondered if that dimple
was what lured her into you.
She needed you.
Needed to use you.
Needed to screw with you.
Maybe that's why you stayed...
The screwing was just so good to you.
When the sun kissed your dimple
through the curtains,
the lamp shade she bought you,
the salvation you thought she gave you,
I almost gave into the thought
that you were healed from the bruises
that she left beneath the left side of your chest.

Infatuation

I love how your humor
leaves imprints on the darkest parts
of my mind.
You could snatch the pessimism
from my vocal box,
if I let you.
Kiss away the
"When I was little" wounds,
and
mark my corpses as
"annihilated"
in permanent ink.
I think you're one of the gems
my play auntie used to talk about...
The few who adore simplicity
and favor stretch marks
that reveal perplex voyages.
The few who adore caressing dreams
and back you up
on goals like 30GB thumb drives.
I lied when I said, "you're alright."
I'd fight for us if there should ever become an *us*.
Not tryin' to rush this...
Just sayin'...
I'd make backtracks to what I said
and apologize quickly...
'Cause, holding your heart is far more
valuable than being right.
Not tryin' to rush this... I'm just sayin'.

Behaved Phoenix

Embers in a cold corner
quietly kissing ashes,
regret and defeat.
Remains of a Phoenix in the early stages
of soaring high and glowing.
Captured in mid-flight--
his destination was to the impossible.
They sent him to hell.
Lassoed his freshly big and bold wings,
lit two matches, one for his tail
and the other,
his beak.
Sent him to chambers his ancestors
used to scream in as he burned brightly.
Threw him in a room, swooned
his family to believe he was causing
a ruckus amongst other beasts.
They left him when his screams
became more of a high whistle.
They smiled at his defeat.
Bolted the door shut.
Embers in the corner-
ashes
scattered everywhere.
When there was nothing left
but wind hushes, he rose out of the ashes.
Flew out of the unbarred window.
He flew low and timid
for the remainder of his life.

She Is Beautiful.

"You're so pretty for a dark-skinned girl,"
she uttered to my friend.
Another friend pretended
she didn't speak such tunneled futility.
I'm not an actor to reality
so, I had to speak as miss dark-skinned beauty
stood there wide-eyed with tears in her eyes.
"Why isn't she beautiful, period?"
The woman looked at me as though six snakes
spewed from my mouth
even though
she was the one releasing venom
from her lips.
She had light brown melanin adjacent
to my own and looked back
as if she wasn't alone.
"Well, I mean, society thinks she is pretty, not gorgeous.
So, it really isn't me you should be asking.
Maybe if she were bald, maybe then she'd be called beautiful."
My heart melted into my stomach
as another Sista openly agreed
with society's folly.
"Yes, by society's standards she is the ugly duckling
but this goddess incarnate is an immaculate swan.
Wrapped tightly in elegance
her flesh reeks of ageless beauty and mystery.

She is beautiful, period."
Society's definition of beauty?
Snip, snip, tuck in, caked on make-up,
suck it up and hair plugs.
All she has to do is wake up,
wash off the eye crust and shrug.
Society's definition of beauty?
Exploitation, grotesque emulation,
applauded fetishes and Botox injections.
It's a filthy checklist that demands
we degrade our stunning imperfections.
A checklist that alternates, choosing
and rejecting which culture to exploit
for a season and go back
to demeaning it when it gets old
The woman stammered in a frantic manner,
"Is it really that deep?"
My friend, rich in melanin, replied,
"Why must your mind be so meek,
compliant and receptive
to whatever the media feeds you?
I am not begging to be
beautiful in everyone's eyes.
I just can't stand the lies
that darker skin is not option.
We're not second-rate beauties,
we are beautiful, period."
The woman walked away shaking her head
and muttered how
mean and angry her kind can be.

Heavy to Carry

She had plans to kiss the sun.
Dunk a few of her friends
and pretend she was a deep-sea diver
or a mermaid in the Nile River.
Plan accordingly.
Prepare for the worst.
Bring your "Yes, Ma'am" &"No, Sir"
for the justified terrorist in blue.
Leave your dignity at home,
honey, they've brought
their egos packed tightly on their belts.
Bring your joyful smile
and don't skimp on the overcast
shame above your braids and crown.
Bring your towel.
Bring your shades.
Maybe you should have left your shade,
your beautiful melanin at home...
It's just too heavy to carry these days.
Your glory is just too
heavy to carry these days.

There you were in your bathing suit
ready to swim only to drown in
your own tears and confusion.
Screams everywhere.
Waves of chaos flooding the streets.
Your braids were divine and they
instantly became rudders to guide them.

What a sight to see, a grown man
assaulting a queen-to-be.
He was just too scared of her glory.
Too alarmed by the faux stories
of royalty with melanin-kissed skin.

Cherry-Colored Casket

He was supposed to hand me a dozen roses
in a mahogany straw basket
but instead,
I'm laying roses on
his cherry-colored casket.
This isn't about the mayhem
due to the recession.
It's the about the degradation of our princes,
the slaying of our successors.
Their crowns were not meant
to be found after their last breath.
I know I'm not the only one
who feels a knot in my chest
every time we hear another
vulnerable gem being killed by armed men.
Justifications as to why
it was fit to kill
the young men in melanin are too eerie.
Placing blanket statements
over living bodies whose ancestors
were lynched with similar justification.
Comfort does more damage than good.
The uneasiness is comforting.
The truth is nauseating.
The deniers are piled up
to the Andromeda galaxy
while finding solutions fall on deaf ears
and willing narcissists to hashtag on social media.

Phoenixes were in training before
they were checked.
This is not chess- It's a slaughter.
No methods or rules.
Kings, Queens and Bishops
are stagnant on making moves.
No one will intercede for our babies,
teens and men...
I can't seem to keep my grandma's voice from cycling
in my head, "Use what ya got.
Don't let your burial plot
shine in vain."
So, I'm using my lil' ol' poems,
hoping they eradicate minds
and annihilate neutrality for such a matter as this.

Ruby

As I sat at my desk
with my arms around my chest poutin',
Grandmama came in the room shouting,
"Gal, you betta quit all that huffin', puffin',
poutin' and start that homework.
Hmph, your generation is doing thangs
my generation only dreamed of."
She shuffled out the door;
I read more about a girl birthing integration.
I realized her worth was more
than the Sancy diamond.
You see, while she dreamed simple things,
her reality conquered venomous
hatred that affected beings.
Beings who couldn't understand equality.
She was just going to school
> ***in her white Mary-Jane shoes.***

She probably dreamt of a Crayola box
full of vibrant colors, illustrating stars
that grinned when she grinned.
Only if she knew that she would
cause temptations of integration.
Only if she knew her caramel brown
would be frowned upon once
she embraced the rebellion to cross the color lines.
What a bad crayon she was
> ***in her white Mary-Jane shoes.***

She probably dreamt
of cookie boxes torn open,
ready for her to eat and sweets
the size of the U.S Marshals who aided
the bombardment of an unjust division.
If only she knew she'd soon curtsy
against the fear of diversity
as she learned her alphabet
> ***in her Mary-Jane shoes.***

She probably dreamt of a big tooth comb
that discreetly passed her hair
without the "oochin' and ouchin'"
or grouchin' around.
Probably dreamt of sun showers
showering upon the dark embrace
that overtook her new school.
Only if she knew her upgraded
education caused hesitation
among masses who prayed for change.
Ruby Nell fell into a reality her ancestors
only dreamed of.
She went to a school which changed a country.
I snapped out of my daydream when Grandmama'
say
"Didn't I tell you to get a moving with that
homework of yours?
You just don't understand, honey,
Your generation is doing things
my generation could only dream about."
I didn't pout
I think I understood then
that dreams are sleeping realities--ready to be risen.

Dear 1960s

Dear 1960s,
We're still bedridden from injustice.
Too reluctant to scream anymore.
White sheets cover our bodies as the masses
are engrossed in plastic entertainment
and slap stick antics.
They tied our hands,
rubbed clay on our ankles
and indicted us for laziness.
Told us to speak our minds
then inclined that we filter
our truth with their cloudy eyes.
So... subtle now.
Honey on their poisonous words.
But, leave the absurd deaths
as identical to yours.
Thank the Lord for the honey, I guess.

Dear 1960s,
They killed your children without repentance.
Disrespected your entire essence-
then quoted scripture
in the same sentence.
Senseless strange fruit hung
on your southern trees,
1960s, nothing has changed.
Except they're quicker
to shoot the babies than to hang.

Quicker to distort the story,
go home with faux glory and a bag of cash.
Forget the truth, I guess.
Still senselessly killing our youth,
armed with skittles, Arizona iced tea and hair brushes.
Those lethal skittles, Arizona iced tea and hair
brushes.

Dear 1960s,
It's haunting to say that nothing has changed
except for technology, hedonistic ideologies
as to why the slow genocide
of deep melanin should remain.
Nothing has changed.
Except there is no need for a hatchet!
The pistol feeds their egos much more quickly.
Whether we're
blessed and highly favored
in our
Sunday best suits, or redundantly
saggin' in our expensive
jeans with the tag hangin' for proof,
we are no longer aloof to the truth that
our attire does not change our demise if racists
want to kill us due to our brown hue.

Dear 1960s,
We don't miss you.
It appears the only difference
is that your television was in black and white.
Ours are in vibrant colors
while the lies are still see-through.

Have a Sense of Humor!

Thursday at around 8:45-ish am,
morning melodies mask
my secret anxieties
of subtle racism in Corporate America.
A faithfully warm November breeze
raises my kanekalon box braids
as I hurriedly walk heavy down hills
of concrete.
Fierce faced, emotionally laced up
to be ***that girl***
for the remainder of my time.
I reflect on yesterday's
ludicrous antics:
She was cackling.
Light snorts of free falling
on appeased ears by the copy machine,
holding many years of life in her bones
her volume at the maximum level,
eyes deep with innocence,
heart the size of seven Nephilims
she said to him,
"I should kick your little smart ass
and then there would be
one less oriental in the world."
He laughed.
Face a tad bit red, jaw line
so tight I could see the
the outline of his teeth, he laughed.

Another co-worker
shot up from his cubicle
wide-eyed, not surprised, hurriedly;
he announced an invitation
for her and him
to walk to the coffee room,
I guess because her joke was so funny.

Because he wanted to compliment her wit,
because even though they already took
their daily walk to the coffee room,
he needed another cup to discuss
with her the beauties of life,
because her joke was too exquisite
for our understanding,
because she is so light-hearted
and color blind
because she hates being politically correct.
Meanwhile,
I write it down and take note of it.
For just in case her amusing lips speak
such eloquence my way.
Fast forward to walking up to the office
and I breathe in deeply.
Waiting to be *that girl* because from my view:
People belittling political correctness
are the ones who have no respect for other people.

The Majority Rant

Arrogant in their ignorance.
They carry their savagery
like it's heaven sent.
Repent for the worst and justify
their actions with the hurt they've felt.
We've dealt with these types of people before.
They're emotionally virulent
while filling their impalpable
wounds with tangible toys.
Devoid of honest intent,
but an abundance of selfishness.
Who knew that faces could look
so plastic today, while substance
fades away into nothingness.
Arrogant in their ignorance of value.
Being "Your Brother's Keeper"
is seen from the rear view.
They give into social media acceptance
like Botox injections.
They give into the temptation
of bullying and then crucify
the victim for speaking up.
The cup of foolishness is running over.
They'd rather take two shots to the face
than disgrace their egos for the benefit of unity.
Usually, this is the part they'd respond to
with refutes that scream
only insults with no weight.

No words for resolution- just hate.
I wait for the vintage perceptions
to trickle back into society like respect for
our fellow human beings and integrity.

Arrogant in their Ignorance

I can't stand bigots and their faux gray hairs

Whispering Alarm Clock

The 21st century never looked so eerie.
A vintage glow,
sort of cream with dingy borders.
Sophisticated vindication for savagery
against unarmed women and men
with melanin.
Primitive hate but updated tactics--It's tragic.
Insidious racism spilling
over the screens
and into receptive minds.
Internal rhyming of the 1940s
with a hint of the 1960s acrostics.
It is now 5 o'clock in the morning.

Unhidden and Unaddressed

Brown eyes, brown skin,
and a healthy afro under a gray brim.
Smiles within
but his eyebrows always cave in.
Perfect attendance
at work and knows his worth.
Takes care of his kids, he is no statistic.
Provides for his household,
holds his lady close.
Doesn't boast about the car
he drives for the money he earns.
Yearns to be the best he can be,
eats well for longevity.
He's always on time, and his crime?
Being in the wrong skin, wrong place,
wrong size, wrong time,
way too much melanin, I guess.
He got the death penalty within a second.
He was in a suspected stolen car:
Red Jaguar with a blue flag in the back.
He was driving a white Expedition
with two cracks
on the turning signal light.
A cop pulled him over
and asked him to step out of the vehicle.
Went as far as searching him
for weapons and drugs.
He found nothing but grocery bags

and fluorescent light bulbs.
The man sucked his teeth
in frustration and shrugged.
The cop heard the aggravation,
dropped a bag of white powder
in the man's vehicle.
The cop looked up and exclaimed,
"What the fuck?"
The man jumped and replied,
"What's wrong?"
The cop pulled out the Ziploc bag
of powder and slammed the trunk.
The cop smiled
and slowly walked towards
the man's direction,
"What do we have here?"
The man's eyes widened
as though he saw an expensive chandelier.
The man shook his head and yelled,
"You are framing me!"
The cop balled up his free fist and swung.
The man ducked and yelled, "help."
The cop then pulled out the gun
and the man's life was done.
The next day the newspaper's read:
EX-JAY WALKER KILLED BY COP FOR RESISTING ARREST.
Usual unhidden and unaddressed story for a man with melanin.

Listen, Lady Phoenix

Listen, Lady Phoenix!
Don't smile because you are uncomfortable.
Don't laugh to prove you are un-bothered.
You are valuable enough to be bothered.
You can look at a nasty utterance
at the lips and call it inappropriate.
You are worthy.
Just as worthy as the person spewing tastelessness.
You are worthy.

When your dreams are equal to a man's,
but you're told to take your place
and be humble.
When you're rebuked to sit back
and let him achieve dreams so big
constellations gossip about it.
Remember,
your vagina wasn't involved
in the matter of your purpose.
Your soul shook you to your core
while you were still sleeping,
painted pictures in your day dreams
of being a lawyer, a bad ass with a smile.
Remember,
your vagina wasn't involved in the matter.

Listen, Lady Phoenix!
Snatch your dreams without feeling the need to

justify.
Your crown is reason enough
to snatch the stars from the sky,
just so the next generation
can see hope during their darkest moments.

During the moments when
you're one of the six brown people
at your job and your cubicle
happens to be surrounded
by co-workers who crack tasteless jokes
and justify themselves by saying,
"Well, everybody is racist,"
and you want to explode from the ignorance,
chew through their
privileged "tongue-in-cheek,"
their half-assed empathy for different
kinds of beautiful,
And
Spit
Them
Out,
and you're torn between
calling them out professionally and appropriately
only to be the angry black woman,
or say nothing and allow them to believe
that their poisonous preference of humor is okay.

No matter what you do:
Don't smile because you are uncomfortable.
Don't laugh to prove you are un-bothered.

You are valuable enough to be bothered,
just as valuable as the person spewing tastelessness.
You are worthy.

When waking up with the desire
to bury the sun because the daylight
is just too damn hard to face,
strugglin' to once again shove yourself
into boxes your family, education and career
have designed for you,
you shudder at the thought
of placing
your cold feet on the hardwood floors
of your bedroom.

Listen, Lady Phoenix!
You were meant to be you.
Just you.
Your crown is reason enough
to snatch the stars from the sky,
just so the next generation can see hope
during their darkest moments.

Mister

You are a coward with an ego.
Got more potential than our black heroes.
Legacy yearns to grow
from your pores but you adore
your idleness and drunken stagnancy.
Mister,
you won't find the remedy in your misery
or changes in your circumstances.

Chaos

Fed into social media acceptance
like Botox injections.
He's guided by his erections.
She's defined empty thrusts as affection.
Intimacy is robbed of its treasure,
vulnerability and overcrowded love language.

BackBiters

The whispers reveal legit insecurity.
Someone, please give the backbiters some tea.
Maybe a remedy to their bad habit.
Every downfall they witness,
they gotta grab it, exaggerate the story
and laugh at it.
Petty conversationalists.
Lost from their individual purpose
they bring down others,
so, they don't feel worthless.
Transparency isn't in their vocabulary.
They can't face their own legendary nakedness.
Too many scars, too many blemishes.
Too troubled to allow optimism
to leak from their sentences.
The whispers reveal legit insecurity.
Someone, please give the backbiters some tea.
Maybe a remedy to their bad habit.
Or duct tape to create some temporary
silence from their venom.
I hope they realize their words can be weapons of
hate or weapons of peace.
I hope they can wake up,
surrender to their own titanium path
and strut down their lovely enlightened road.

The Quiet Ones

A voice, frozen and timid,
bellows from the base of my belly.
My words,
black and white,
are seen yet never heard.
Absurd pedestals
and selfish eyes are the reason
for my disguise.
A voice, frozen and timid,
bellows from the base of my belly.
Opening wounds, but could never
be soothed by a listening ear.
No one wants to hear about
the dying butterfly who merely
wanted to soar towards love and
give it back to those who are empty.
Plenty of people like me.

> **We're like glass green houses
> yet no one can see through
> us.**

We've decided to let the weeds grow tall.
Allow the moss to take over the walls.
Makes no sense to let anyone
in if you know they're not listening.
There are various cracks
in our walls from the rocks thrown

after we've shown love
to those willing to take it.
We give our dandelions and white lilies,
even though
we're wallowing in the wind...
Bending but never breaking.
A voice, frozen and timid,
bellows from the base of my belly.

Turn of Events

I was in my pinstripe suit
walkin' up 5th avenue,
during the midday.
All eyes were on me
and I could see my soft sashay
and mellow flow
had the fellas' wantin' ta
do a no show
at their jobs.
I felt like a bird soaring
high in the sky,
until an actual bird flying high in the
sky pooped on my head.
I saw my crush across the street
and he said,
"Oh snap, Jazzy got pooped on!"
I decided at that very moment
that I'd live in a cave and change my name
to Dave Lancaster.
Yes, Dave Lancaster.

For the Carefree Mornings...

I feel light.
Like shower vapors escaping
underneath the bathroom door
into the hallway,
and vanishing into nothingness.

I feel light.
Like the 5 am aroma of the bakery truck.
Its sugary scent leaving its trail
on the messed-up streets of Dekalb Avenue.
Open windows and flared noses surrender
to the odor of cakes,
macaroons and tunes of old school Soca.

I feel light.
Breathing in deeply.
Fresh air and that garbage truck!

Dear Lord,
what the hell do we throw away these days?
Exhale, exhale, exhale!
Hold my breath until the master of stench leaves.

I still feel light.
Like a dandelion seed floating
through NYC
and its fast-paced everything.
Spinning in mid-air to and fro,

brushing past victorious business women
in lavish suits, sticking on freshly
gel downed hair of the man
selling used cars
that should've been put down
    2,000 miles ago.

I feel light.
Observing the coffee-sucking vampires
vivaciously telecommunicating
with the arrogantly stubborn customers
and the passively-rude consumers.
Bless God for cubicles and boundaries.
Thankful for my green tea
and
serenity's energy humming
ever so gently wrapping
its transparent mist
around my fingertips.

I feel light.
Remembering that every day is just
one footprint to the massive journey
we are all destined to reach.

Diane

She is electrifying, divine and complete.
She *is* essentiality.
She *is* unique.
Bodaciously captivating.
Infinitely inspiring.
She is irrepressible.
Silence is her servant
and her voice can still chaotic hearts.
She is alluring.
The singing siren
ain't got nothin' on her sultry.
Poetry bows down to her.
Heck, she birthed creativity!
She *is* divine.
Never guided or controlled by time.
Artists flow to her direction.
She invented royalty and sparks.
She is the morning epiphany and the evening closure.
She doesn't have to keep composure, she *is* elegance.

Ms. Lady

I'm inspired by you, Ms. Lady.
Lately I have been thinking
about the ways you say your dreams
to the world so effortlessly like ABCs.
Always boisterous and classy.
You're sassy with your soul
and nurture it with the good stuff
I'm sure Nefertiti rubbed her scalp with.
<u>Hot damn,</u>
I love the way you do you the way you do it!
I'm inspired by you Ms. Lady.
Your voice reminds me
of what I'm missing beneath
the left side of my chest.
Your hum motivates my core
to find healing within
and confront the madness of self-sabotage.
You must be a mirage!
You're too sultry
and sweet, too empathetic and deep.
Pure ebony divinity sitting next to me
and all I can do is glare in awe.
I'm inspired by you Ms. Lady.

Raine

You're a hidden gem that's meant
to blind the arrogant
and humble them back to the middle.
Little girl, your voice
is meant to be heard
and your spunk is intentional.
Please shine on.
Illuminate the lives around
you like the North Star.

Raine,
Please rain down your platinum
persona on the ones who need it most.
Don't boast about your light
to the haters, leave them to be spectators.
You're beautiful and flaw-fully perfect.
Always know you're worth it.
You're a hidden gem that's meant to blind
the arrogant, and humble
them back to the middle.

Bashir

Piercing eyes on canvas,
oil painted finesse in a 70s dream of classy funk.
Black elegance on a flat never looked so good.

Let Go

Forgive the monsters
who are afraid of their own reflection.
Your confidence in your own
beautiful mess is too intimidating for them.

The Morning After

After rinsing off a sin
that felt like freedom in bucketfuls.
After redeeming my voice
from his oppressive words
and iniquitous hands.
After peacefully understanding
that there was nothing left to do but cease his future
to be unchained from our past.
The morning after, I peeled the covering
off what I thought was a figment of my imagination-
Me.
Last night, I saw **Me.**
Bursting through my caste-iron skin,
screaming towards the sky and glistening peace
from within.
I saw **Me.**
Hidden beneath his scars,
my mother's reflection,
the masses' eyes and shameful haze;
I saw **Me.**
And, damn it, it was beautiful.
In all my painful, dark, murky watered tears,
I saw **Me.**
Originally kissed by love and sensitive heart beats,
I saw **Me.**
The morning after...
After I persuaded winter to coat
his steady heart and still his blood stream.

I look at my reflection,
proud of the transgression that freed me.
Eyes blood shot red, I fed my anger
and saw an escape last night.
I look to my left at the light peaking
through the summer curtains.
I'm certain his body is still floating
in my neighbor's pool.
A hint of drool sits on my chin.
I feel queasy the morning
after my freedom-filled sin.
My freedom-filled sin.

Grass Ain't Finna Be Greener

Blue girl in a red dress swinging
her hips on a tabletop,
diamond on her left hand
but still looking for the right one.
"Sing to me, baby."
She says
to the man
with gator feet
and a golden grimy grin.
A stack of cash in one hand
and a stolen knife in his pocket.
Her thin
legs and big heart would fit just right on his belt.
Narcissistic strut and stern glances
as he watched her dance.
He wrapped his thumb
and index finger around one of her ankles.
She looked down, blushed,
and brushed off his grasp.
She jumped off the table
and they began to dance.
Two-stepping
on hot coals and rickety chances.
This is a ludicrous lust not true romance.

Diamond on her
left hand but still
looking for the right one.

Six months
later she's pawning
her diamond, roaming
the streets barefoot
and vulnerable.
Screaming out,
"Sing to me, baby."
Looking for her
new fella with
the golden grimy grin.
He took all her money
and all her celebratory gin.

Blue girl in a black dress
shuffling down
the concrete jungle with bundles of trinkets to sell.
She finally saw
her car with her new
fella's wife in the driver's seat.
Her new fella peeped her on the corner.
She yelled out,
"Sing to me, Baby."
He quickly
looked straight ahead
and tapped a notch on his belt.

Dominique

You live courageously,
wish somebody would,
and got tenacity that would
make the egos of men shake.
You're authentic.
You have *100% in your face,*
I got yo back, I'm here for your grace.
That family first, old fashion poise
that gives hope for boys, that yes,
Queens still exist.
You just don't carry the royal pompous persona.
But you sashay like Isis
and walk like Nefertiti.
Strength like Horus
and game like Aphrodite.
Hmph,
these brothas better not take your dopeness lightly.

Annie Ruth

Wisdom lost a keeper of its secrets.
York children lost a mother.
Valley Stream lost the queen of good grass
and pretty decorations, sittin' on concrete
steps that were faithfully swept.
The prettiest flowers out in the front,
swaying in the wind as though
they were finna see their
favorite singer sing their favorite tune.
That southern dialect totin',
unruly-child-snatchin',
love givin' lil' lady with dimples
deep enough to hide in,
is no longer here.
Queen of sass imprinted within her veins.
Straight talka embedded on her tongue.
Fussy in god-like heels with footsteps
birthed out of humility.
   You can't tell me my Grandmother left quietly.

Pieces of wise tales hidden in her scriptures.
Story tellin' truths and fables
underneath her laugh.
She wasn't a flame,
 she was a wildfire at its peak--all the damn time.

Peace introduced her entrance.
Steady shufflin' house slippers followed suit.

She gave her heart without hesitation to her family,
even during the times, she should have been selfish.
She had nice China.
She had nice silverware.
She had nice rugs.
She had nice black statues
holding the fort in her living room.
Had to tiptoe around the exquisite trinkets,
hold ya breath around the delicate picta frames.
Bet not break her good stuff.
Bet not sit on the good furniture.
Bet not eat up all the food.
Be considerate.
Pay attention.
You can't tell me my Grandmother left quietly.

She was wildly faithful to her old westerns.
Our eyes glued to the television,
when she was 73 years old,
crackin' peanut shells
and challengin' my comfort zones.
A wash rag over her shoulders
when it was a bit chilly.
One wrapped over my heart
whenever life reminded me, it wasn't fair.
She'd say,
"It never is, but ya gotta keep walkin'."

I used to rise up early in the mornin'
to eavesdrop on her phone conversations
with Ms. Pringle or Ms. Mamie.

They'd talk about storms, sensationalism,
church affairs, and marital ones too.
Those *mhms* always tempted me
to get the popcorn out of the top cabinet in the kitchen.
But I'd lay quietly in my bed and listen.
Sometimes I wondered if she knew.
Because at the end of those conversations
she'd always spew out some golden nuggets
that were easily interpreted for me to grasp.
   You can't tell me my Grandmother left quietly.

Ma!

Your big, beautiful, butter brown eyes
can snatch the F from fierce,
pierce through
foolishness as though your eyes
knew how to get Freddy,
as though you knew how to make Jason flinch,
as though you knew the secrets of all evils.
You got the "Don't play with me" glare
when I used to talk back, down packed,
tightly sealed and ready to be delivered.
Mommy, best to believe I'll say what I want…
under my breath, of course.

You believed in me before I was
even aware of my lil' ol' glow,
before I even knew how to spell purpose,
before I was scootin' my lil' booty
down the steps in diapers,
before I could even crawl on the 638 wooden floors,
before I was kickin' in that belly of yours.
You believed in lil' ol' me.
I know.
Your eyes always tell me so.
But I guess that's how it's supposed to be
for Queens like you.
Foreseeing destinies, nurturing hearts
before doctors could hear heartbeats.

I remember the day
you taught me that Langston Hughes poem
and about Angela Davis--
about Ruby Bridges, about Marcus Garvey,
and about Billie Holiday.
Oh, and Diana Ross, and
the black legacies that never
seem to be uttered in over-crowded
NYC classes
and uninterested teachers.
Your lips spoke of the creatures of night,
the lurkers who ate the good souls of men
who never knew of conviction.
I thank God for you…

My first teacher of where I came from,
my motivation for where I wanna go.
The Yemoja in my eyes,
soul spilling over integrity--
Miss good lookin' lady.
The Zipporah I look at in the mornings.
Sandra, your everything is beautiful.
Bursting with possibilities,
your heavy feet speak hope.
Your arms swing perseverance
when you walk.

But I guess, that's how it's supposed
to be for Queens like you.
Hidden gems that blind Jezebels
when light touches the corner

of your dimensions.
You illuminating diamond,
you pain bearing
storytelling, forgiving and cultivating soul.

I love you so….
I love you so…

Secrets

I grew up forbidden to listen to secular music.
So, I snapped my fingers
to Billie Holiday in corners,
shook my shoulders to
The Fugees discreetly,
and wiggled my widdle hips timidly
to the Red Hot Chili Peppers.
My forbidden love was dancing.
To kiss the ground
with the pitter-patter of my feet,
arms flailing rebelliously, was peace to me
in a heart-shaped bottle.
I was madly in love with the un-godliness,
I suppose.
The beats made my face
light up like I was attempting to beat
Chris Griswold's record.
One night, in '95,
as my father was driving me
to my grandparents' house,
I remember kicking my feet in the air
and giggling under the passing streetlights.
No, they were spotlights
highlighting my big twists and pastel-colored
barrettes,
shaking to the under beat
of a Biggie Smalls' record.
My daddy glanced for a moment

and smiled.
His eyes fixated back on the Bay Ridge streets,
smile still frozen on his face- he was proud.
Bopped his head too,
verbally underlined my moves--
giggling, he said,
"Okay, Princess. Ya gettin' down."
Suddenly...
I froze.
Shoulders raised up,
hands gently crossed
over my thighs,
I thought of my dancing prohibition at home and
sighed.
His smile never left.
Whenever I made decisions
based on my heart's desire
and my love for all, he'd smile.
When going through animosity
for being me without shame, he'd smile.
He'd smile at my early
beginnings of knowing what this life is all about.

To the Wonder Women Clan

Hands...
speaking quiet discomfort,
long days and many fulfilled goals.
Hands...
carrying scents of victory
and
everyone seems to pass by their triumphs
that build legacies
with just a piece of their intellect.
But I never pass by The Wonder Women Clan
without remembering what their smiles look like just
before they execute what they initially saw as
impossible.
I've seen them build bridges
within tornadoes
and still had time to laugh
and buy trinkets at knickknack shops.

This poem is for the Professor Lockes':
Who listen to discernment's whispers like 1920s
layman reading yellow journalism on their lunch
breaks.
Her plants grow gardens
and she creates sheroes out of introverts and
pessimists.
She's too preoccupied with living
to reflect on her impact.
But I do.

I take her burden of reflecting proudly.
Eyes widen at the Formicidae
that enter her office as ants
and leave as fiery creatures ready
to take on this realist world.
> This poem is for the Mrs. Ciklics':
> who are keepers of peace whenever hurricanes
> run through deep ruminations without warning.
> Murphy's Law doesn't rule her.
> She's got Murphy by the colla', juggling more
> responsibilities than a mother of seven.
> She knows what wisdom tastes like
> and never criticizes its bitter-sweet taste.
> She's too busy lassoing sunrises to show
> us how bright we can potentially
> shine when we walk heavy.

But I pick up the time for her.
Hold tightly to the hourglass
and snatch up every proverb that falls from
her fingertips after attempting
to add body to her already dope hair.
> This poem is for the Ms. Wines':
> Whose voices are the origin of hope
> and carry syllables on their tongues
> that remind us that God is not finished
> with us if we keep moving.
> She can spot a snake from 65,000 miles away
> and hear its hiss in her sleep.
> She speaks of order.
> Grabbing chaos by its boot straps
> and dragging it to the siren gods.

She can't look up to see how far she's come.
She's too busy living lavishly fearless,
and dangerously in love with other beautiful hearts,
to look behind at her footsteps.
But I do.
I put my little foot over her footprints.
Gracefully understanding that I will never have her
strength but enough to carry my own path.

This poem is for the Wonder Women Clan
who are fueled by coffee,
who promote peace, take no shit
and sashay with whatever life gives them.
To the Wonder Women Clan...

How I'm Doin'

I don't know much
but I know joy.
I don't know much
but I know peace.
I don't know much
but I know everything
falls into place in its time.

I was ashamed of my own shadow.
Too embarrassed to sneak glances
when sunlight blared sidewalks
barely watched my silhouette
through my peripheral--I was damaged.
Couldn't manage to address my truth,
guarded by scriptures and proud self-shaming.
Kissed everyone else's dreams
when I couldn't even hold the hands of my own.
Couldn't even whisper them into pillows.
The fresh silk sheets were intimidating.
'Cause I thought Phoenixes were
unworthy to love themselves,
too tainted to adore their feathers,
too distinct for self-acceptance
and too worthless
to own their own sentences.

Then, one day, a lightning bolt struck my essence…
Welcomed me to gaze upon

my black silhouette on pavement.
I snatched the invitation.
And I silenced the rainstorms-
no longer rocked to and fro.
Solidified my being, eradicated the worthlessness.
Lit up the flaws, gifts, talents, and experiences.
I cried out half-hearted self-love
like New Jersey flash floods.
I began to love me as if I never knew of shame.
Smiled at flaws like first sights on sunrises.
I was at peace with my everything.

    I don't know much
     but I know joy.
    I don't know much
     but I know peace.
    I don't know much
    but I know everything
    falls into place in its time.

Used to whisper my questions of oppression
'cause I was taught that my transgression
was too great to even hold a syllable.
Born to be unworthy
due to the actions of the Eden couple.
Joy was snatched from underneath my heels,
dangled two inches away from me.
Clutching my bible for insight,
ignoring my heart
for it was biblically deceitful.
Shamed my God-given desires,
muzzled my authentic persona

for overly-anxious rumination
and I am not talking about self-denial.

Then one day...
At my doctor's office struggling to breathe,
sucking in albuterol, heaving
out Grandma smoker wheezes-I felt it.
Authentic presence that was too big to box
and I shared the moment with an Islamic woman.
Then another with a Buddhist
and another with an agnostic.
I let go of my childhood religious rhetoric.
Threw out the hectic need to
feed my mind with upgraded legalism.
I found joy.
The overcast of forced love cleared.
I am here, in this moment.
Catching stillness with my ears.
Listening to my intuition
like it was my best friend.
Love without feeling the need
to 'cause Jesus says so.
I love 'cause I want to.
Give 'cause it's in my heart to.
Be me without the need
to be boxed in or indoctrinated.
My smiles are real now.
I don't know much
but I know joy.
                I don't know much
                but I know peace.

> I don't know much
> but I know everything
> falls into place in its time.

My wings stretch out without
fear of being misunderstood.
My beak is un-muzzled.
No book controls me.
No past hurts derail me,
I smile inwardly, show love externally.
At peace during rainstorms,
know joy even when I am burning brightly,
'cause I know now that everything will fall into place.

Let's Connect!

www.jasminefarrell.com
Instagram: @justbreathejasmine
Twitter: @authorjfarrell

Use #PGAGD with quotes from the book.

If you loved the book and have a moment to spare, I would appreciate a short review as this helps new readers find my content.

www.ingramcontent.com/pod-product-compliance
Lightning Source LLC
Chambersburg PA
CBHW030042100526
44590CB00011B/300